Seven Keys to Successful Mentoring

D0567720

IDEAS INTO ACTION GUIDEBOOKS

Aimed at managers and executives who are concerned with their own and others' development, each guidebook in this series gives specific advice on how to complete a developmental task or solve a leadership problem.

LEAD CONTRIBUTOR	E. Wayne Hart
CONTRIBUTORS	Craig Chappelow
	Cynthia D. McCauley
	Douglas Riddle
	Clemson Turregano
DIRECTOR OF PUBLICATIONS	Martin Wilcox
EDITOR	Peter Scisco
ASSOCIATE EDITOR	Karen Lewis
DESIGN AND LAYOUT	Joanne Ferguson
CONTRIBUTING ARTISTS	Laura J. Gibson
	Chris Wilson, 29 & Company

CCL No. 443
ISBN No. 978-1-60491-061-2

CENTER FOR CREATIVE LEADERSHIP
WWW.CCL.ORG

Seven Keys to Successful Mentoring

E. Wayne Hart

Center for
Creative
Leadership®

THE IDEAS INTO ACTION GUIDEBOOK SERIES

This series of guidebooks draws on the practical knowledge that the Center for Creative Leadership (CCL®) has generated, since its inception in 1970, through its research and educational activity conducted in partnership with hundreds of thousands of managers and executives. Much of this knowledge is shared—in a way that is distinct from the typical university department, professional association, or consultancy. CCL is not simply a collection of individual experts, although the individual credentials of its staff are impressive; rather it is a community, with its members holding certain principles in common and working together to understand and generate practical responses to today's leadership and organizational challenges.

The purpose of the series is to provide managers with specific advice on how to complete a developmental task or solve a leadership challenge. In doing that, the series carries out CCL's mission to advance the understanding, practice, and development of leadership for the benefit of society worldwide. We think you will find the Ideas Into Action Guidebooks an important addition to your leadership toolkit.

Table of Contents

EXECUTIVE BRIEF

Mentoring is an intentional, developmental relationship in which a more experienced, more knowledgeable person nurtures the professional and personal life of a less experienced, less knowledgeable person. Both mentors and mentees realize many benefits from mentoring, as do organizations that encourage, structure, and support mentoring. Effective mentors develop the leadership capacity of their mentees while increasing their own skills. They transfer their knowledge and expertise back into their organizations. They nurture the alignment between employee aspirations and organizational imperatives, and they create depth and loyalty within their organizations. Leaders who take mentoring seriously and handle it effectively have a profound impact.

What Is Mentoring?

Mentoring is an intentional, developmental relationship in which a more experienced and more knowledgeable person nurtures the professional and personal life of a less experienced, less knowledgeable person. Typically, a mentor has been in an organization or profession longer and has greater authority within the organization or profession than does a mentee. The combination of expertise and position enables a mentor to have significant impact on a mentee.

Mentoring relationships are developmental because they promote experiences that motivate individuals to learn and grow, expose them to learning opportunities, and provide support for the learning and growth. In many cases such relationships are mutually developmental, for mentor and mentee alike. Mentoring can be an informal process agreed to by the parties, or it can be formalized as an organizational initiative, with organizational structuring and monitoring, and organizationally aligned goals.

In order to further clarify the role and actions of a mentor, it may be helpful to differentiate mentoring from other developmental relationships. For example, performance outcomes are a primary focus of leaders, and their capacity to achieve those outcomes rests heavily upon the authority of their positions. The primary focus of a mentor is development of an individual with an eye to organizational outcomes; the capacity of the mentor to influence rests heavily on his or her ability to relate in a nonauthoritative way while, paradoxically, guiding the mentee from the perspective of a superior position and expertise. These differences have implications for organizational politics and interpersonal communications.

Mentoring can also be differentiated from its closest cousin, coaching. Mentoring has a different focus and range of functions. While coaching typically focuses on enhancing current job performance, mentoring focuses on career path. Mentors typically use coaching skills a great deal as they endeavor to guide a mentee; in this regard they manage the relationship, guide and counsel, motivate and inspire, serve as models, and rely heavily on questioning and listening skills. However, mentors also leverage their positions to sponsor mentees for developmental experiences and to survey the environment for threatening forces and opportunities. They leverage their expertise to transfer knowledge.

The Importance of Mentoring

Leaders realize many benefits from mentoring, including personal satisfaction and fulfillment, enhanced creativity and professional synergy, career and personal rejuvenation, development of a loyal support base, and recognition for developing talent.

People who are mentored also gain many benefits: access to leadership opportunities, career mobility, better rewards, increased adaptability when facing new situations, improved professional identity, greater professional competence, increased career satisfaction, greater acceptance within their organizations, and decreased job stress and role conflict. Additionally, mentees enjoy some of the credibility and influence of the mentor through association.

Now's the Time

Optimizing talent through mentoring is timely. Given that Generation X is smaller in number than the retiring Baby Boomers, organizations are recognizing a shrinking pool of suitable candidates for succession to leadership positions. Organizations face an impending leadership vacuum. Good leaders will be scarcer. Competition to attract and retain good people will be fiercer. Developing and retaining talent is critical to organizational success now.

Organizations also benefit from mentoring. It helps them attract talent, and it enhances organizational commitment among employees who seek developmental opportunities. Turnover decreases, and development accelerates. Typically, mentors have a well-developed view of organizational direction and dynamics, which they impart to mentees, and can better align a mentee's efforts with organizational objectives, enhancing organizational capacity. Many contemporary organizations consider mentoring a key competency among their leaders.

What Mentors Do

A successful mentor acts on behalf of a mentee, with an eye to the well-being of the organization or profession. In the service of that mission, successful mentors

1. develop and manage the mentoring relationship
2. survey the environment for threats and opportunities
3. sponsor the mentee's developmental activities
4. guide and counsel
5. teach
6. model effective leadership behavior
7. motivate and inspire

As you read about and reflect upon these functions, keep in mind that they are appropriate in different amounts in different relationships. You do not have to "do it all" in order to be a mentor. But as a mentor, you may be called upon to perform any or all of these functions. It depends on the needs and wants of your mentee, as well as what works for you. The following sections will inform you about what is involved with each function so that you can better prepare yourself to mentor someone in your organization or profession.

1 Develop and Manage the Mentoring Relationship

Mentoring relationships start in different ways. Formal programs in organizations, for example, often match a mentor with a mentee based on wide-ranging criteria. In such cases you may be assigned a mentee; you may or may not have much say in the matter. Other formal designs create tentative pairings and permit mentor and mentee to get acquainted and determine whether they think they will work well together before designating the match as final. Organizations sometimes host mixers where potential mentors and mentees can meet each other; mentors or mentees may be told to seek out a partner. You might find yourself contemplating a mentoring relationship through informal opportunities as well. Someone may approach you and ask you to mentor him or her. You may spot someone who shows great potential and initiate a conversation with him or her. Or you may feel a personal calling or need to help someone else develop and then deliberately look for a suitable person. However your mentoring relationship gets started, there are some key points to keep in mind as you develop the relationship.

A fundamental consideration is that mentoring is collaborative. It's not something you do to someone; it's an activity you do with someone. The mentor and the mentee share responsibility for the success of the process. Successful mentoring stands on a foundation of rapport, collaboration, respect, trust, and commitment. To create that foundation, you should address aspects of the mentoring relationship such as readiness, selection, getting acquainted, building trust, setting goals, self-disclosure, and monitoring. You should approach these aspects of the relationship from a collaborative perspective—that is, you and your mentee are jointly responsible for how things turn out. The following sections address topics that will help you develop and manage a mentoring relationship:

- your readiness to be a mentor
- selecting a mentee
- getting acquainted with your mentee
- self-disclosure
- building trust between your mentee and yourself
- handling the power differential between your mentee and yourself
- setting goals together
- monitoring the mentoring process and mentee follow-through
- clarifying expectations
- potential pitfalls of the mentoring experience

Readiness. If you are considering being a mentor, your first consideration should be whether you are ready. Mentoring can be an intense, personal, long-term relationship, so you must be ready and willing to commit your time and attention and to make yourself available. There may be implications to being a mentor in your organization or profession at any given time. The questions on page 12 will help you determine your readiness. As you reflect on these questions, it can be helpful to discuss your responses with a trusted colleague who can serve as a sounding board.

Consider getting some training that will help you feel more comfortable and be better prepared to serve as a mentor. You may want help improving your communication skills or influence style, for example. You may want to better understand what constitutes a developmental experience for someone. You may want to build greater confidence in your ability to perform the mentoring functions discussed in this guidebook.

If you are already mentoring someone, the question of readiness is whether you're ready to take on another mentee. How many

Mentor Readiness Questions

Reflect on each of these questions as you consider mentoring someone in your organization.

1. How do you feel about being a mentor?

2. What benefits would you gain from being a mentor?

3. What would it cost you to be a mentor?

4. Do you have time to mentor someone?

5. Is this a good time for you to mentor?

6. Can you make a long-term commitment to this process?

7. How comfortable are you having a collaborative relationship (not an authoritative one) with a person less experienced and influential than yourself?

8. Do you understand the functions and methods of mentoring, and do you have the skills to perform them?

9. What organizational implications will you face if you mentor?

10. Do you have sufficient long-term support, such as ongoing training, for your role as a mentor?

would be too many? There is no absolute answer to this question. Your answer would depend on your total workload and scope of responsibility. Most leaders during the peak productivity years of their careers can barely find the time to mentor one person, let alone several. However, more senior leaders, transitioning to a slower pace, have the breadth and depth of experience to be marvelous mentors and may have more time. For such people, serving three or four mentees may be workable. The key here is to ask yourself how many mentees you are ready for at this point in your career. If you are ready for more, take them on one at a time. Give yourself a chance to find out how each new relationship is going to flow before making the next commitment.

Selection. If you've decided that you're ready to mentor, the next thing for you to consider is the person you will mentor. The selection process varies. In cases where an organizational initiative manages the process, the human resources department may identify potential mentors and mentees, often basing decisions on nominations from senior leaders. Then, using specific matching criteria, HR pairs mentors and mentees. Even better, an organization may also have the prospective mentor and mentee get together to determine their comfort in working together. In cases where no organizational initiative exists, mentors and mentees sometimes find each other in informal ways. Other informal situations involve a broker, who connects people in a mentoring relationship.

Whatever the selection process, a key factor to successful mentoring is a good fit between the mentor and person mentored. Success doesn't necessarily come from pairing mentor and mentee on the basis of such criteria as working in the same function, coming from similar backgrounds, or the mentor's working at the level or in the function to which the mentee aspires. To determine whether you and your prospective mentee are a good match, also examine communication skills and style, ambition, initiative, intelligence, loyalty, shared interests, common aspirations, and other characteristics.

If you experience a poor fit with a potential mentee, discuss it with the mentee and any key stakeholders. Those discussions should emphasize a no-fault perspective on your part. That is to say, stress that there is nothing wrong with the mentee. Place your emphasis on the factors that suggest a poor fit to you. You may even find yourself at a loss for words about how to describe the poor fit. Don't let that stop you. Consider talking with a trusted colleague or advisor about your reservations; such discussions might help you develop clarity and strength of your convictions or find an alternative that enables the mentoring relationship to move forward.

Below is a list of fit considerations. You can use this list to speculate about whether there is likely to be synergy between you and the prospective mentee:

- value systems: being compatible in terms of work-life balance issues, polarizing political or religious convictions, people orientation versus task orientation, moral and social norms and standards, ethical perspectives

- aligned aspirations: striving for similar things, such as quality, professionalism, social responsibility, justice

- subject matter commonality: knowing about or having an interest in each other's areas of expertise (a physicist and an engineer might work better together than an HR specialist and an engineer)

- attitude or interactional style: feeling comfortable around each other

- compatibility of work management styles: being able to discuss and work with any differences that exist in your styles (directive and authoritative, transformational, collaborative, laissez-faire)

- time factor: having a time limit for the mentoring engagement (you may have greater tolerance for a marginal fit)

Getting acquainted. If you do not know your prospective mentee well, arrange two or three occasions to spend time together. Ideally, you would hold your first meeting in a business setting. Subsequent meetings could be held in less formal settings. It might also be helpful for you to observe your prospective mentee in organizational situations, such as during a business meeting or as he or she instructs a direct report. Questions to keep in mind during these early meetings include the following:

- Am I comfortable being myself around this person?
- Do I like and respect this person?
- Can I be an effective advocate for this person?
- What can I offer this person that is of developmental value?
- Am I confident that this mentee will demonstrate good judgment and behave professionally?
- Is the prospective mentee ready to do his or her part in the relationship? Is it the right time for this person to be mentored?

The key question in getting acquainted is, Who is this person I'm dealing with? You need to find out the mentee's strengths, weaknesses, aspirations, behavioral predispositions, and the kind of impact the mentee's behavior has on other people. There are several ways you can gain a fuller picture of your mentee.

- Formal assessment methods such as personality profiles and developmental surveys (360-degree feedback instruments, for example) may be available through your organization's HR department. Discuss these tools with your mentee and determine whether the results can be shared (different organizations have different rules about this). If you are not certified at interpreting such reports, ask your HR department for support.
- Interviews with coworkers, friends, former bosses, teachers, coaches, and family members may be helpful. Seek

15

permission from your mentee before you do any interviewing. Draw up a list of questions with your mentee.

- Direct conversations with your mentee can also be a rich source of information.

- Observing your mentee in action can reveal critical information. Watch how he or she acts during a sales calls, for example, read a report he or she has written, or note how he or she connects with others during informal encounters.

Use the Mentor Relationship Assessment to pull together your observations and the results of your interviews and conversations. Remember that throughout this early stage of the process—and, in fact, all the way through the mentoring process—you and your mentee should continue to ask whether you're right for each other. Research and anecdotal reports suggest that mentoring relationships arranged on the basis of logical considerations are less successful than mentoring relationships that at the outset establish an affinity between mentor and mentee.

Mentor Relationship Assessment

How would you describe the person you will mentor in regard to these characteristics?

- strengths, aspirations, values
- biases, blind spots, weaknesses, vulnerabilities, fears
- self-awareness, self-image
- perception management skills
- receptivity to and use of feedback
- habits for managing the balance of work, renewal, and non-work priorities
- interests, involvements, hobbies, and important relationships outside of work, including community connections and leisure activities
- readiness to be mentored
- receptivity to a mentor like yourself

Self-disclosure. Revealing who you are enables your mentee to develop a realistic understanding of you, often shedding idealized notions of who you are that typically lead to disillusionment down the road. It also provides models for what to do, and what not to do, in addressing a variety of life situations. Finally, it enables a mentee to connect with you at a deeper level, to develop trust, and to open a broader scope of topics for discussion.

Share your experiences, successes, and failures, describing what you learned and how you used them to develop into a better leader. From those stories, mentees learn to recognize, face, and effectively manage their predispositions, fears, apprehensions, and struggles. Share how you feel about situations and how you manage those emotions, especially how you channel negative reactions into constructive action. Discuss your hopes and concerns about the future, as well as your regrets and gratitude about the past.

The question of how much to share and how often comes up frequently. It is hard to say. Remember that mentoring is about the mentee, so don't tell stories just to hear yourself talk or to revel in reminiscing. When you reveal something about your own life, it should be for a purpose, such as giving your mentee permission to take certain action; helping your mentee feel normal about his or her thoughts, feelings, or actions; showing your humanness; or demonstrating a way of doing or not doing something.

Building trust. As a mentor, it's important for you to start building trust between yourself and your mentee during the selecting process and while you're getting acquainted—and to continue building trust throughout the course of the relationship. Among other things, building trust requires that you be consistently genuine, friendly, open, approachable, encouraging, reliable, accountable, honest, and ethical. Trust encourages your mentee to become more assured in taking risks, more confident in achieving a successful outcome, and more comfortable asking for advice and assistance. Mentees rise to meet the expectations of mentors when the relationship between them is characterized by mutual trust, support, and respect. Guidelines for creating that trusting relationship include

- providing affirmation of your mentee's uniqueness and worth as an individual, including abilities, intentions, potential, judgment, and achievements
- affirming current superior performance
- advocating reasonable risks
- remaining calm when errors occur
- staying true to agreements and commitments
- giving honest, direct, caring, and prompt feedback
- vetting any assessment or investigation plans with your mentee before taking action
- getting your mentee's side of stories before forming conclusions
- listening actively and assuring your mentee that you understand from his or her perspective
- being candid about your own agenda and letting your mentee know why you are doing what you are doing
- setting clear agreements about confidentiality

Handling the power differential. Because you will have greater seniority and/or expertise than your mentee, one of the factors to manage is the difference in power between you. A mentee will experience your perspectives as authoritative and typically be inclined to defer to you. He or she will recognize your relatively greater influence within the organization and may hope you will use it in specific ways. Others may expect you to have greater influence over your mentee than you actually have and therefore greater responsibility than is realistic. You will do well to remember, therefore, that anything you do may be interpreted through the lens of that difference in power. You will have to set clear boundaries for yourself and your mentee about expectations and degrees of freedom for both of you.

Remember to empower your mentee to be proactive in establishing this. Suggestions in the sections on clarifying expectations and potential pitfalls will be helpful to you in this regard.

In order to cultivate the kind of collaborative relationship that characterizes the best mentoring relationships, you likely will strive to influence with rational persuasion, collaboration, consultation, and inspirational appeals. However, remain alert that these tactics may be perceived as pressure because of the power differential. You may get compliance when you hoped for commitment. You will want to keep the unequal power issue in mind as you clarify expectations with your mentee and others.

Setting goals. Another important aspect of building a solid mentoring foundation is setting goals. You and your mentee should define your expectations and set goals that align with your mentee's aspirations and with organizational imperatives (such as strategic direction and operational priorities) and realities (such as how much time you have to work with your mentee). You may see greater possibilities for your mentee than he or she sees. If that's the case, encourage your mentee to set higher goals than he or she might otherwise set. If you discover that your mentee is unrealistic about what can be achieved, discuss different possibilities and work toward an agreement. In working toward consensus, keep these things in mind:

- Base goal setting and expectations on a realistic assessment of circumstances.
- Encourage ambitious goals that challenge your mentee.
- Convey encouragement ("I see you as capable of this," for example).
- Gently shed light on unrealistic aspirations.

Monitoring. Once the mentoring relationship is up and running, you will want to monitor how things are going for you as a mentor, for your mentee, and for the mentoring process in general.

19

You may want to keep a journal of your mentoring experience or have periodic conversations with a trusted advisor, noting your adjustment to and satisfaction with the mentoring process. Ask yourself questions such as the following:

- How are the mentoring process and my mentee like what I was expecting, and how are they different?
- What am I getting out of the mentoring process, and how does that compare with what I was expecting?
- What is most satisfying and most unsatisfying about the mentoring experience?
- How do I feel about continuing the mentoring process for another three, six, or twelve months?

You can use these same questions to ask your mentee about his or her adjustment to and satisfaction with the mentoring process.

Another monitoring activity is to take some time with your mentee and review the progress made toward mentoring goals and expectations. You can guide your discussion with these questions:

- Are we on track and on schedule with progress toward our original goals and expectations?
- Have any significant circumstances that have implications for the mentoring process changed since we started?
- Have our goals and expectations changed, or do they need to be redefined?

Clarifying expectations. You will be well served by discussing and agreeing with your mentee about what you expect of each other, what each of you is committed to doing, and the limits of your commitment. Some leaders may feel that all the tasks of mentoring add up to an overwhelming project. If you find yourself thinking this, remember that you are free to pick and choose which tasks to perform and the extent to which you perform each one. Be honest with yourself and your mentee about what feels right for you, where your limits are, and how you will address unexpected demands on your role when they show up. Similarly, urge your mentee to be honest with you about what he or she is committed to doing and where his or her limits are.

That said, there are some expectation issues worthy of comment here so that you'll have a chance to think about them in advance.

- Your accountability as a mentor. Will you be held accountable by anyone, and for what? Your boss may have expectations of you and want progress reports. Your mentee may also hold you accountable. If your organization has formalized a mentoring program, there may be a program stakeholder keeping an eye on progress. Be sure you have clear agreements with anyone who will hold you accountable. Use the functions of mentoring outlined in this book as a guideline for identifying and agreeing to what will be on the accountability list and what will not. Beware of being held accountable for things you cannot control, like your mentee's performance, how others perceive and treat your mentee, or changes in the organization or industry that impact the process. You should consider accepting responsibility for performing specified mentoring functions at defined levels.

- Guaranteeing enough interaction. With all the demands of your and your mentee's jobs, it will be challenging to have enough interaction. Planned meetings will get scuttled at the last minute because of business emergencies. Meetings may be postponed because one or both of you have been unable to perform a follow-up task from the previous meeting. Meetings may be forgotten. Geographical distances and different time zones complicate the picture. Further, there is no absolute standard for what is enough interaction. Telephone sessions might be sufficient at some points but not at others. E-mails can keep momentum up when telephone or face-to-face sessions are impractical. Make this an ongoing point of discussion with your mentee. What is frequent enough interaction to keep momentum going? Your boss or a stakeholder for a formal internal program may have expectations about this as well. Every case will be unique. Be proactive in planning and assessing this aspect of the experience.

- Confidentiality. There are things that come up in the mentoring process that should not be kept confidential and things that are negotiable. Threats or intent to harm someone else, to misrepresent the organization to others, to give away organizational secrets, to commit theft, to lie, and to perform unethical actions are examples of issues that are not protected by confidentiality. Negotiable issues include a mentee's misgivings about staying in the organization, strong negative reactions a mentee has to another person or organizational policies and changes, and performance input to the mentee's boss or a formal program stakeholder. Discuss this and reach clear agreements with your mentee and anyone who may hold you or your mentee accountable for the process.

Potential pitfalls. Finally, as you engage in and manage a mentoring relationship, be forewarned that there are threats to be aware of so that you can recognize and address them if they surface. If they do, it's time for a straightforward talk with stakeholders about limits and expectations. Get it out on the table without taking a judgmental or adversarial position. Create a collaborative discussion to decide how to move forward. Common pitfalls include the following:

- The mentee becomes overly dependent or disengaged.
- A superior or peer, or someone mentoring another person, becomes suspicious or competitive with respect to the effort you are devoting to your mentee.
- A poor decision or action by your mentee reflects badly on you.

- You find yourself in a conflict of interest between what seems best for the organization and something different that seems best for your mentee.
- You are perceived as unfairly favoring your mentee as compared with other, equally qualified people.
- You are seen as overreaching the tolerance of your organization for mentors to advocate on behalf of mentees.
- Senior management is unsupportive or disruptive of the mentoring process.
- The mentoring process derails.

2 Survey

A mentor's second function is keeping a watchful eye on the environmental horizon, looking for threatening organizational forces (such as rumors about or distorted accounts of your mentee's behavior, shifting organizational priorities, and reorganization) as well as positive opportunities. Here are some things to be on the lookout for:

- rumors
- people taking an adversarial position relative to your mentee
- shortcuts through the system
- low-visibility or no-win assignments, high-visibility or win-win assignments
- bureaucratic entanglements
- potential conflict with colleagues, potential synergies with colleagues
- unjust criticism

Surveying the environment means being alert even when you are not actively involved with your mentee. It involves having your mentee's welfare in the back of your mind most of the time. You must be capable of and adept at recognizing threats early, before they impair your mentee's performance or reputation, the organization, or the mentoring relationship. The same is true of opportunities so that there will be time to make the most of them.

Once you have spotted threats or opportunities, you can apply other mentoring functions such as sponsoring, guiding and counseling, and teaching to empower your mentee to address these issues successfully.

3 Sponsor

The third of the seven functions of a mentor involves advocating on behalf of your mentee, sponsoring him or her for appropriate opportunities. Your mentee's work and organizational environment will provide many opportunities and resources for learning and advancement. As a mentor, seek ways to connect your mentee with situations that provide visibility and development. Advocate for your mentee by recommending him or her for new, high-visibility positions or assignments through which your mentee's contributions and achievements can demonstrate his or her capabilities to peers and bosses. Opportunities include

- working on important accounts
- participating on influential committees
- leading a project that entails considerable interface with influential stakeholders
- membership in professional organizations
- arranging access to meetings that would otherwise be closed
- introductions to key people in the organization or profession

As a mentor you should be engaged in these activities yourself. Demonstrate your connection with different constituencies and your belief in the value of such engagement. Also be aware of the pitfalls unique to this function. Once you advocate on behalf of your mentee, your reputation is on the line for how he or she performs. That's a lot of responsibility, especially if you have very little influence over the circumstances that will determine success or failure for your mentee.

4 Guide and Counsel

The fourth function of a mentor is guiding and counseling. From time to time, mentees seek the counsel of mentors for personal issues—matters that go beyond career and organization. To meet this need, you need to be comfortable dealing with your mentee's emotions, patient in exploring factors that may drive your mentee's actions, and respectful of your mentee's past experiences. You play the role of a trusted confidant in such matters. You can be a dialogue partner in helping your mentee assess personal issues and challenges, and you can be a source of support as he or she gains clarity on those issues and develops options. Counseling may involve personal issues:

- challenging and supporting by confronting dysfunctional biases, attitudes, or other predispositions
- challenging poor decisions or impulses
- assessing life balance and burnout issues
- supporting "taking care of self" actions

Your role as mentor might also involve counseling your mentee as to how to handle environmental situations that you observe or about which you learn through keeping a watchful eye on events around you (see previous section on surveying). Your counsel could involve helping your mentee do these things:

- better manage the impressions others are forming of him or her, thus managing rumors and unjust criticisms

- be more alert to and skilled at dealing with political and personal adversaries and conflicts with coworkers
- take advantage of shortcuts through the system and maneuver around bureaucratic entanglements

Be watchful, however, and remain aware of your limits. There are no topics that are off limits for discussion. However, some personal issues can surface that likely will fall outside your training or comfort zone. Examples of such issues include drug or alcohol problems, family or marital problems, and anxiety or depression. In such cases, you should recommend professional help. In addition to that recommendation, you can be supportive by being a good listener, sharing your own similar experiences, or venturing an "if it were me" suggestion. Most often, your informal counseling skills may be required when mentees

- have problems, difficulties, and concerns with developing professional competence and career satisfaction
- question their career path
- are unsure of success and fear failure
- struggle to manage professional and organizational relationships
- face difficulty balancing career and personal life
- experience personal blocks to navigating organizational culture, politics, power, group norms, and systems

5 Teach

The transfer of skills is a key motivator behind formal and informal mentoring programs. Teaching is the fifth function of a mentor; it means showing your mentee how to do something, questioning, and listening, all with an eye on keeping your mentee focused on priorities and oriented toward action. It may call on you to create or seek out challenging assignments for your mentee, while remembering that his or her competencies will evolve across several stages of developmental skill. Teaching consists of

- continually assessing competencies, performance, and personal needs, attitude, and well-being
- identifying and reaching alignment with your mentee on developmental and skill-based goals and objectives that challenge him or her
- designing challenging assignments that help your mentee move toward the ultimate goal
- checking to see that challenges fit the needs of the person you're mentoring (for example, a task that fits an introverted individual who is not socially inclusive might not be right for someone who is gregarious and socially inclusive)
- supporting the person you mentor by sharing relevant experiences from your career and life and also relating accounts of others' successes and failures
- giving information, resources, and direct training
- providing correction for inappropriate behaviors (for example, underperforming, inattention to detail, maintaining too narrow a perspective, working inefficiently, unethical or unprofessional conduct)
- helping your mentee see inevitable errors that occur during the learning curve as developmental steps
- helping your mentee manage anxiety
- giving honest and caring feedback

Mentors need to be patient and systematic thinkers, linking opportunities with the development of skill and capacity.

6 Model

Your mentee can often learn by observing how you handle situations. Modeling is the sixth function of a mentor. Mentees notice things like confidence, competence, professionalism, and standards. Through observation, they can learn how to cope and how to most effectively handle a situation. Often, this kind of learning isn't consciously planned, but it can be. Opportunities for modeling that can be deliberately created include the following:

- inviting your mentee to participate in activities and deliberately observe you

- discussing your mentee's observations of you in various situations

- encouraging your mentee to participate with you in various situations, such as a project team, brainstorming sessions, or conflict management events

Being a model of coping is quite different from being a model of excellence or mastery. Each has its place. Also, mentors must be selfless in their modeling efforts. Leveraging the power of modeling must be done for the good of your mentee, not for your own self-gratification or for appreciation or recognition from your mentee.

7 Motivate and Inspire

Helping mentees align their actions and goals with their values, passions, and sense of personal efficacy supports them in their development. It often falls to the mentor to awaken the creativity and innovative ideas in the people they work with and to help them articulate their strongest potential. To perform the seventh function of mentoring, you can use various tactics for motivating and inspiring, which include the following:

- making it safe for your mentee to brainstorm with you
- affirming creative efforts
- modeling creativity and innovation
- providing a supportive realism for overly expansive or unrealistic thinking
- asking questions and listening for what is important to your mentee
- encouraging and facilitating new perspectives
- reminding your mentee that there are multiple right answers to questions and solutions to problems
- supporting the quest for continuous improvement

Mentors have to be optimistic and creative themselves. They must practice visions of greater outcomes for their mentees, their organizations, and themselves. And they must be open to—even in search of—unforeseen opportunities and outcomes.

Final Thoughts

Leaders who have not developed mentoring skills may function very well in such leadership activities as setting direction, aligning actions, and motivating people. But they will fail to fully transfer their knowledge and expertise back into the organization and to nurture the alignment between employee aspirations and organizational imperatives. Leaders who mentor effectively create depth and loyalty within the organization. They help employees and organizations realize their hopes for each other.

People often learn not by themselves but through others. As a mentor, you have an opportunity to help develop the leadership capacity of another person while you increase your own skills in such areas as managing relationships and providing feedback. If you take mentoring seriously and handle it effectively, your impact can be profound. Along with parents, teachers, classmates, coaches, and bosses, you will take your place in your mentee's line of positive developmental influences.

Suggested Readings

Baldwin, D., & Grayson, C. (2004). *Influence: Gaining commitment, getting results.* Greensboro, NC: Center for Creative Leadership.

Johnson, W. B., & Ridley, C. R. (2004). *The elements of mentoring.* New York: Palgrave Macmillan.

Lombardo, M. M., & Eichinger, R. W. (1989). *Eighty-eight assignments for development in place.* Greensboro, NC: Center for Creative Leadership.

McCauley, C. D. (2006). *Developmental assignments: Creating learning experiences without changing jobs.* Greensboro, NC: Center for Creative Leadership.

Ragins, B. R., & Kram, K. E. (Eds.). (2007). *The handbook of mentoring at work: Theory, research, and practice.* Thousand Oaks, CA: Sage Publications.

Ting, S., & Scisco, P. (Eds.). (2006). *The CCL handbook of coaching: A guide for the leader coach.* San Francisco: Jossey-Bass.

Wei, R. R., & Yip, J. (2008). *Leadership wisdom: Discovering the lessons of experience.* Greensboro, NC: Center for Creative Leadership.

Yukl, G. (2009). *Leadership in organizations* (7th ed.). Upper Saddle River, NJ: Prentice Hall.

Background

CCL's research and educational experience since the 1970s repeatedly point to the importance of on-the-job relationships in career development. Both personal capacities and effective connectedness with other leaders are enhanced by a variety of such relationships, including mentoring, coaching, peer relationships, and action learning collaboratives. Benefits and pitfalls have been found in informally established relationships, as well as in formal ones in which an organization takes an active role in initiation and implementation. CCL has learned key success components of such relationships.

Building upon this understanding, CCL published *Formal Mentoring Programs in Organizations: An Annotated Bibliography* in 1997. Researched and written by Christina Douglas, this publication goes beyond literature review to highlight best-practice considerations for design and implementation of mentoring programs. CCL's experience and learning about challenges and contributions of mentoring across racial, gender, ethnic, and hierarchical differences have been elaborated in its *Handbook of Leadership Development* (1998, 2004). Additionally, CCL has designed training programs that apply what we have learned about developing leaders to mentoring assignments.

This guidebook fills a small gap in CCL's publications on the subject by focusing on the mentor and what the mentor does. In addition to what we have learned about mentoring per se, it incorporates what we have learned about leadership development and developmental relationships.

Key Point Summary

Mentoring is an intentional, developmental relationship in which a more experienced and more knowledgeable person nurtures the professional and personal life of a less experienced, less knowledgeable person. Mentoring relationships are developmental—in many cases, for mentor and mentee alike. Mentoring can be either a formal or informal process. Both mentors and mentees realize many benefits from mentoring, as do organizations that encourage, structure, and support mentoring.

A mentor acts on behalf of a mentee, with an eye to the well-being of the organization or profession. In doing so, a successful mentor performs most or all of seven functions. First, the mentor develops and manages the mentoring relationship, keeping these key points in mind: his or her readiness to be a mentor, selecting a mentee, getting acquainted with the mentee, self-disclosure, building trust, handling the power differential, setting goals together, monitoring the mentoring process and mentee follow-through, clarifying expectations, and the potential pitfalls of the mentoring experience.

The mentor also surveys the environment for threats and opportunities, keeping his or her mentee's welfare in mind. The mentor sponsors the mentee's developmental activities, advocating on behalf of the mentee and recommending him or her for appropriate opportunities. Mentors also guide and counsel, teach, model effective leadership behavior, and motivate and inspire. These functions are appropriate in different amounts in different relationships.

Leaders who mentor effectively transfer their knowledge and expertise back into their organizations. They nurture the alignment between employee aspirations and organizational imperatives, and they create depth and loyalty within the organization. They help employees and organizations realize their hopes for each other. Mentors help to develop the leadership capacity of their mentees while increasing their own skills. If they take mentoring seriously and handle it effectively, their impact can be profound.

Ordering Information

TO GET MORE INFORMATION, TO ORDER OTHER IDEAS INTO ACTION GUIDEBOOKS, OR TO FIND OUT ABOUT BULK-ORDER DISCOUNTS, PLEASE CONTACT US BY PHONE AT 336-545-2810 OR VISIT OUR ONLINE BOOK-STORE AT WWW.CCL.ORG/GUIDEBOOKS.

CPSIA information can be obtained at www.ICGtesting.com
Printed in the USA
LVOW02s1155300914

406506LV00018BA/39/P